Forever Young **Diet**

TARLA DALAL
India's # 1 Cookery Author

S&C
SANJAY & CO.
MUMBAI

Third Printing : 2006

Copyright © Sanjay & Co.

ISBN : 81-86469-97-4

RRP : £3.99

Published & Distributed by : **Sanjay & Company**

353/A-1, Shah & Nahar Industrial Estate, Dhanraj Mill Compound,
Lower Parel (W), Mumbai - 400 013. INDIA.
Tel. : (91-22) 2496 8068 ● Fax : (91-22) 2496 5876 ● E-mail : sanjay@tarladalal.com

Distributed in U.K. by : **Mr. Deepesh Chotai**

Gifts By Vishaldeep, 378 Romford Road, Forest Gate, London, E7 8BS
Tel : 0208 4700486 ● Website : www.vishaldeep.com ● Email : info@vishaldeep.com

Recipe Research & **Production Design**	**Nutritionists**	**Photography**	**Designed by**
Pinky Chandan Dixit	Nisha Katira	Jignesh Jhaveri	Satyamangal Rege
Pradnya Sundararaj	Sapna Kamdar		
Arati Fedane			
	Food Styling	**Typesetting**	**Printed by :**
	Shubhangi Dhaimade	Adityas Enterprises	Minal Sales Agencies, Mumbai

INTRODUCTION

We all yearn to stay forever young — in body, mind, spirit and looks. This book ensures fitness and well-being through its innovative and nutritionally balanced recipes, planned specially for those who are health conscious and want **"to be young"** from within. Unlike cosmetic makeovers, which only touch the surface, eating wisely works from within by building up your health so that your body becomes more resilient to the ageing process.

We have divided the book into 5 major sections viz recipes **For Glowing Skin, For Shining Hair, For Bright Vision, For Healthy Bones and To Increase Immunity.**

I, along with my team of chefs and nutritionists have exclusively planned **37 recipes** that are not just healthy but very tasty as well. We have included only natural ingredients and used simple cooking procedures so that all the nutrients are retained. Each recipe has a **nutritive value table** that highlights its main nutrients.

With its **total diet plan**, this book will not only help you feel young, but look young too.

Here's to a forever youthful you!

Regards,

5

CONTENTS

For Glowing Skin

One of the greatest treasures that we can have is **healthy radiant skin**. The skin excretes waste products, absorbs moisture and protects from infections. If the balance of the skin is disturbed it can result in dryness, excessive oiliness and inability to protect against infections.

The natural and best way to begin would be by following a healthy-living plan that would include regular outdoor exercise, enough rest and sleep, sensible stress management, drinking pure water, and most importantly, a nutritious diet.

Each nutrient in a well-balanced diet plays an essential role in keeping the skin healthy and youthful.

- **Protein** has the major tasks of building and maintaining the skin cells.
- **Iron** helps to ensure a proper supply of blood, oxygen and other nutrients required for the maintenance of the skin cells.
- If the skin is protected from getting dry, it is thanks mainly to **Vitamin A.**
- Performing a similar function is the group of **vitamin B-Complex**, which also prevents the appearance of brown spots, mainly on the face, forearms and legs.
- **Vitamin C** assists in retaining the freshness of the skin and making it glow.
- **Vitamin E** uses its antioxidant properties to prevent the skin from getting discoloured and wrinkling.

The minerals **Calcium** and **Zinc** help to protect the skin and keep it healthy.

Protect, nurture and cleanse your skin with these recipes to keep your skin glowing and charming....

8

✳ Skin Glow Soup ✳

A *delicious soup rich in calcium and vitamin A to treat your skin with an extra glow.*

Preparation time : 10 minutes.   No cooking.   Serves 4.

2 cups roughly chopped cucumber
3 to 4 tbsp mint leaves
2½ cups thick fresh curds (dahi)
salt to taste

Blend all the ingredients in a blender. Add a little cold water if the mixture is too thick. Refrigerate and serve chilled.

Nutritive values per serving
Energy : 158 calories
Protein : 5.8 gm
Carbohydrate : 8.4 gm
Fat : 8.2 gm
Calcium : 276.3 mg
Vitamin A : 248.6 mcg

❄ *Strawberry Banana Smoothie* ❄

*T*ry this vitamin C and calcium rich yummy recipe, which is indeed a natural blusher for your glowing skin.

Preparation time : 5 minutes.   No cooking.   Makes 2 glasses.

1½ cups milk
½ cup chopped strawberries
2 tbsp honey
½ cup chopped banana
a few drops vanilla essence
a few ice-cubes

For the garnish
a few slices strawberries

1. Mix together all the ingredients and blend in a liquidiser to get a thick smoothie.
2. Pour the smoothie into 2 tall glasses and serve garnished with a few slices of strawberries.

Nutritive values per glass
Energy : 340 calories
Protein : 8.2 gm
Carbohydrates : 48.0 gm
Fat : 8.1 gm
Vitamin C : 26.5 mg
Calcium : 349.0 mg

❊ Sprouted Fruity Bean Salad ❊

Sprouting increases B-complex vitamins of the beans... when tossed into a salad with fruits, it helps to freshen up your skin.

Preparation time : 20 minutes.   Cooking time : 30 minutes.   Serves 6.

1 cup mixed boiled sprouted pulses (moong, moath beans, chana etc.)
¾ cup chopped apples
½ cup orange segments
2 tbsp cut grapes
2 tbsp sliced white radish
¾ cup chopped salad leaves
½ cup chopped spinach (palak)
1 tsp finely chopped green chilli (optional)
salt to taste

To be mixed into a dressing
¾ cup thick fresh curds (dahi)
2 tbsp chopped mint leaves

1 tsp sugar
salt to taste

1. Mix all the ingredients for the salad.
2. Just before serving top it with the dressing and refrigerate.
   Serve chilled.

Nutritive values per serving
Energy : 88 calories
Protein : 3.7 gm
Carbohydrate : 12.2 gm
Fat : 2.1 gm
Folic acid : 16.4 mcg
Vitamin B_3 : 0.1 mg
Zinc : 0.2 mg

❋ Carrot and Green Peas Sandwich ❋

A *colourful and easy way to provide your skin with lots of protein and vitamin A.*

Preparation time : 5 minutes.   Cooking time : 2 to 3 minutes.
Makes 2 sandwiches.

4 brown bread slices, lightly buttered
1¼ cups parboiled and finely chopped carrot
¼ cup green peas, boiled and slightly mashed
2 tbsp grated paneer (cottage cheese)
½ tsp cumin seeds (jeera)
¼ tsp finely chopped green chillies
2 tbsp chopped coriander
1 tsp oil
salt to taste

1. Heat the oil and fry the cumin seeds until they crackle. Add the green chilli, vegetables, paneer and salt.
2. Cook for 2 to 3 minutes.

3. Spread the mixture on 2 bread slices evenly. Cover with the remaining 2 bread slices.
4. Cut into two and serve.

Nutritive values per sandwich
Energy : 205 calories
Protein : 6.3 gm
Carbohydrate : 28.6 gm
Fat : 7.2 gm
Vitamin A : 1024.7 mcg

❋ Spinach and Carrot Broth ❋

A *palak delicacy enriched with wheat germ to make up for the necessary vitamin A and E.*

Preparation time : 5 minutes.　No cooking.　Serves 4.

2 cups chopped spinach (palak)
¼ cup chopped onions
½ cup chopped carrots
1 tsp cornflour
2 cups milk
2 tbsp wheat germ
1 tsp butter
salt and pepper to taste

1. Heat the butter in a non-stick pan, add the onions and sauté for 2 minutes, till the onions turn transluscent.
2. Add the carrots and cook over slow flame for another 2 mintues.
3. Add the spinach, 1 cup of water and cornflour and bring the mixture to a boil.

16

4. Add the milk and wheat germ and simmer for 5 minutes.
5. Blend in a liquidiser to get a smooth purée.
   Serve immediately.

Handy tip : Wheat germ is readily available at super markets, provision stores and also at chemist shops.

Nutritive values per serving
Energy : 172 calories
Protein : 7.2 gm
Carbohydrate : 12.7 gm
Fat : 7.9 gm
Vitamin A : 1515.9 mcg
Vitamin E : 1.4 mg
Zinc : 0.2 mg

✻ *Orange Sesame Tabbouleh* ✻

Picture on facing page.

Vitamin C rich orange and parsley helps to absorb iron (required for supplying blood to your skin) from bulgur wheat and sesame seeds.

Preparation time : 15 minutes.   Cooking time : 10 minutes.   Serves 4.

1 cup bulgur wheat (broken wheat)
1 tbsp grated orange zest
2 tbsp toasted sesame (til) seeds
2 spring onions, chopped
½ cup chopped tomatoes
½ cup finely chopped parsley
2 tbsp lemon juice
2 tbsp olive oil
2 tbsp orange squash
salt to taste

ORANGE SESAME TABBOULEH : Recipe above ↦

1. Cook the bulgur wheat in 1½ cups of water for 10 minutes till it is tender.
2. Drain and pour cold water over to cool the bulgur wheat.
3. Drain again and keep aside.
4. Combine all the ingredients in a bowl and mix well.
5. Refrigerate for at least 1 hour before serving so that all the flavours blend well.

Handy tip : While grating the orange zest, be careful not to be grate the white pith, as it is bitter.

Nutritive values per serving
Energy : 225 calories
Protein : 4.8 gm
Carbohydrate : 36.7 gm
Fat : 6.7 gm
Vitamin C : 30.2 mg
Iron : 3.2 mg

✳ Tortilla with Refried Beans and Tomato Salsa ✳

A *Mexican delicious recipe full of flavour and colour is best to treat your skin with protein and calcium.*

Preparation time : 15 minutes.   Cooking time : 25 minutes.   Makes 6 tortillas.

For the tortilla
¾ cup maize flour (makai ka atta)
¼ cup plain flour (maida)
1 tsp oil
salt to taste

For the refried beans
1 cup rajma (kidney beans), soaked overnight
1 cup chopped tomatoes
1 clove garlic, crushed
1 green chilli, finely chopped

½ cup chopped onions
½ tsp chilli powder
½ tsp roasted cumin seed (jeera) powder
1 tsp sugar
2 tsp oil
salt to taste

For the tomato salsa
1 cup chopped green tomatoes
1 spring onion, chopped
2 cloves garlic
½ tsp cumin seeds (jeera), roasted
1 green chilli, chopped
1 tbsp chopped coriander
salt to taste

Other ingredients
¼ cup chopped spring onions
¼ cup grated carrots

For the tortilla
1. Mix the flours, oil and salt and make a dough by adding enough warm water.
2. Knead the dough well and keep for ½ hour. Knead again.
3. Depending on the diameter you require for the dish, roll out the dough into 6" (150 mm.) or 9" (225 mm.) diameter thin rounds with the help of a little flour.
4. Cook lightly on a tava (griddle) and keep aside.

For the refried beans
1. Drain the rajma, add the tomatoes, garlic, green chillies, half the onions and cook in a pressure cooker till tender. Drain and keep the drained water aside.
2. Heat the oil in a pan and fry the remaining onions for ½ minute.
3. Add the rajma, chilli powder, cumin seed powder, sugar and salt and cook for 2 to 3 minutes.
4. Mash the mixture coarsely.
5. If it is dry, add some drained water. Keep aside.

For the tomato salsa
Combine all the ingredients in a blender and grind into a coarse mixture. Keep aside.

How to proceed
1. Take a tortilla and spread one portion of the refried beans.
2. Top with 2 tsp tomato salsa, 1 tsp spring onions and 1 tsp grated carrots.
3. Fold into a semi circle and serve immediately.

Nutritive values per tortilla
Energy : 113 calories
Protein : 4.4 gm
Carbohydrate : 17.4 gm
Fat : 2.9 gm
Calcium : 67.6 mg

For Shiny Hair

If we want our hair to look it's best, we've got to feed our body the vitamins and minerals our hair needs to be strong and healthy. What the nutrients do is, literally, strike at the roots. A luxuriant mop of hair can grow only if the roots are properly nourished.

For our hair to really be our 'crowning glory', we need to pamper it, care for it, and feed it properly. Here's how…

- We would require **proteins** to help strengthen our hair.
- **Iron** is important for proper blood circulation so that the other nutrients reach the hair and keep it healthy.
- The mineral **zinc** helps to reduce or even prevent hair loss.
- Among the vitamins, the group of **vitamin B-Complex** does wonders in giving the hair gloss, colour and thickness, all of which are so essential to the appearance of our hair.
- **Vitamin C** ensures the health of capillaries supplying blood to hair follicles.
- **Vitamin E** promotes hair growth and maintains overall healthy hair.

* Protein Packed Poha *

A *combination of sprouts and poha that's simply brimming with protein, vitamin B_3 and iron.*

Preparation time : 10 minutes.   Cooking time : 10 minutes.   Serves 4.

1½ cups jada poha (beaten rice flakes)
1½ cups mixed sprouts (moath beans, moong, red chana), boiled
½ tsp mustard seeds (rai)
¾ cup finely chopped onions
1 to 2 green chillies, chopped
¼ tsp turmeric powder (haldi)
2 tsp sugar
3 tsp lemon juice
1 tsp oil
salt to taste

For the garnish
2 tbsp chopped coriander

26

1. Place the poha on a sieve and wash lightly. Drain and leave aside for 10 minutes.
2. Heat the oil in a non-stick pan and add the mustard seeds. When they crackle, add the onion and green chillies and sauté till the onion turns translucent.
3. Add the mixed sprouts, turmeric powder, sugar and salt with approx. ½ cup of water and sauté for 3 to 4 minutes.
4. Add the poha and lemon juice and mix well.
   Serve hot garnished with the chopped coriander.

Nutritive values per serving
Energy : 153 calories
Protein : 4.7 gm
Carbohydrate : 29.6 gm
Fat : 1.8 gm
Iron : 5.4 mg
Vitamin B_3 : 0.2 mg

* Jacket Potatoes with Broccoli and Red Pepper *

You will love this innovative way of serving calcium and vitamin C rich dish needed for growing hair.

Preparation time : 5 minutes.   Cooking time : 12 minutes.   Serves 4.

4 large potatoes, boiled with the skin on
salt to taste

For the filling
1 cup finely chopped broccoli
1 cup finely chopped red pepper
3 cloves garlic, finely chopped
3 green chillies, finely chopped
2 tsp cornflour mixed with ¼ cup milk
1 tbsp butter
salt and pepper to taste

For topping
2 tbsp grated mozzarella cheese

For the filling
1. Heat the butter in a pan, add the broccoli, red pepper, garlic and green chillies and sauté for 2 to 3 minutes.
2. Add the cornflour mixture, salt and pepper and simmer till the sauce thickens.
3. Remove from the fire.
4. Add the cheese and mix well.
5. Divide the mixture into 8 equal portions.

How to proceed
1. Cut each boiled potato into 2 halves horizontally.
2. Scoop the potato halves, using a spoon so that a depression is formed for the filling.
3. Sprinkle salt on each potato half and fill with a portion of the filling mixture.
4. Top with some grated cheese.
5. Repeat with the remaining potatoes, filling and cheese.
6. Bake in a pre-heated oven at 200°C (400°F) for 5 to 7 minutes til the cheese melts. Serve hot.

Nutritive values per serving
Energy : 132 calories
Protein : 3.5 gm
Carbohydrate : 20.1 gm
Fat : 4.2 gm
Calcium : 69.1 mg
Vitamin C : 66.5 mg

❋ *Gobhi Paneer Palak Parathas* ❋

These unusual, yet delicious parathas are all in one with loads of zinc vitamin A and C for shiny hair.

Preparation time : 20 minutes.   Cooking time : 15 minutes.   Makes 4 parathas.

For the dough
1½ cups plain flour (maida)
1½ cups whole wheat flour (gehun ka atta)
1 cup chopped spinach (palak)
1 tsp lemon juice
1 tsp oil
1 tsp salt

To be mixed into a stuffing
½ cup grated cauliflower
½ cup crumbled paneer (cottage cheese)
2 tbsp chopped coriander
1 to 2 green chillies, chopped

¼ tsp finely chopped ginger
salt to taste

Other ingredients
1 tbsp oil for cooking

For the dough
1. Blend the spinach and lemon juice with 2 tbsp of water in a liquidiser.
2. Sieve the flours with the salt. Add the ghee and mix well.
3. Add the spinach mixture and knead to a semi-soft dough by adding enough water.

How to proceed
1. Divide the dough into 4 portions.
2. Roll out one portion of the dough into a 75 mm. (3") diameter circle and put about 2 tsp of the stuffing in the centre.
3. Seal the edges and roll out again into a thick paratha of 150 mm. (6") diameter.
4. Cook on a hot tava (griddle) on both sides using a little oil until brown spots appear on the surface.
5. Repeat for the remaining dough portions and stuffing to make 3 more parathas. Serve hot with fresh curds.

Nutritive values per paratha
Energy : 235 calories
Protein : 8.1 gm
Carbohydrate : 30.6 gm
Fat : 9.0 gm
Vitamin A : 1170.0 mcg
Vitamin C : 12.5 mg
Zinc : 1.0 mg

✳ *Spicy Bean and Tomato Soup* ✳

The ever-popular tomato soup enriched with protein and iron rich rajma giving strength to your hair.

Preparation time : 10 minutes.   Cooking time : 20 minutes.   Serves 4.

1 cup cooked rajma (kidney beans)
½ cup chopped onions
1 tsp chopped garlic
4 cups chopped tomatoes
¼ tsp chilli powder
1 tbsp chopped basil
½ tsp oregano
½ tsp sugar
1 tbsp oil
salt and pepper to taste

For the garnish
4 sprigs of basil

1. Heat the oil, add the onions and garlic and cook till the onions are translucent.
2. Add the tomatoes and chilli powder and cook for few minutes.
3. Add 3 cups water and simmer till the tomatoes are cooked.
4. Blend the mixture in a liquidiser. Strain.
5. Add the rajma, basil, sugar, oregano, salt and pepper.
   Serve hot garnished with sprigs of basil.

Nutritive values per serving
Energy : 120 calories
Protein : 4.5 gm
Carbohydrate : 15.9 gm
Fat : 4.7 gm
Iron : 2.2 mg

❊ *Avocado Salad* ❊

Picture on facing page.

Vitamin E rich ingredient- avocado creatively tossed in to a salad with honey
dressing rich in zinc.

Preparation time : 20 minutes.   No cooking.   Serves 6.

1 large avocado, sliced
2 capsicums
2 tomatoes, deseeded
8 to 10 pieces baby corn
2 cucumbers

To be blended into a dressing
4 tbsp honey
1½ tbsp lemon juice
2 tsp finely chopped mint leaves
½ tsp crushed pepper
salt to taste

AVOCADO SALAD : Recipe above ➜

1. Gently peel and slice the avocado. Keep aside a few slices for decoration.
2. Cut the capsicum, tomatoes, baby corn and cucumber into big long strips.
3. Blanch the baby corn in boiling water for a few minutes. Drain.
4. Mix all the vegetables and the avocado slices in a large plate.
5. Add the dressing and put in the refrigerator.
   Serve cold decorated with the remaining avocado slices.

Nutritive values per serving
Energy : 175 calories
Protein : 3.0 gm
Carbohydrate : 17.3 gm
Fat : 11.3 gm
Vitamin E : 1.1 mg
Zinc : 0.8 mg

❊ *Methi Palak aur Makai ki Roti* ❊

Nutritious version of traditional makki ki roti packed with vitamin C and iron exclusively for your shiny hair.

Preparation time : 10 minutes.   Cooking time : 20 minutes.   Makes 4 rotis.

1½ maize flour
¾ cup chopped spinach (palak)
¼ cup chopped fenugreek (methi) leaves
2 green chillies, finely chopped
2 tsp sesame seeds (til)
½ tsp salt
2 tsp oil for cooking

1. Mix the maize flour, spinach, fenugreek leaves, chilli powder, green chillies, sesame seeds and salt. Add hot water and make a soft dough.
2. Divide the dough into 4 equal parts.
3. Spread a damp cloth on a wooden board and flatten one part until it is 150 to 175 mm. (6" to 7") in diameter.

2. Lift with the cloth and put it upside down on a tava. Remove the cloth.
5. Cook on both sides, using a little oil. Repeat with the remaining dough to make 3 more rotis.
    Serve hot.

Nutritive values per roti
Energy : 78 calories
Protein : 2.2 gm
Carbohydrate : 9.5 gm
Fat : 3.5 gm
Vitamin C : 6.6 mg
Iron : 0.7 mg

* Khus-Khus ke Parathe *

Khus-Khus rich in iron and zinc is made into a stuffing for parathas and wheat germ is added for its high vitamin E content.

Preparation time : 10 minutes.   Cooking time : 15 minutes.   Makes 4 parathas.

For the dough
1½ cups whole wheat flour (gehun ka atta)
2 tbsp wheat germ
½ tsp kalonji (onion seeds)
salt to taste

For the stuffing
4 tbsp khus-khus (poppy seeds)
¼ tsp asafoetida (hing)
2 tsp cumin seeds (jeera)
4 big red Kashmiri chillies
4 cardamoms (elaichi)
4 cloves (laung)

2 sticks cinnamon (dalchini)
½ tsp chopped ginger
½ tsp kalonji (onion seeds)
2 tsp ghee
salt to taste

Other ingredients
1 tsp ghee for brushing

For the dough
1. Sieve the flour very well.
2. Add the ghee, kalonji and salt and prepare a stiff dough for paratha by adding water. Knead well.

For the stuffing
1. Soak the khus-khus in very little water and make a thick paste of it.
2. In a tava, roast the asafoetida, cumin seeds, chillies, cardamoms, cloves and cinnamon for 2 minutes. Powder the roasted spices very well. Keep aside.
3. Heat the ghee in vessel and fry the ginger and kalonji for ½ minute.
4. Add the khus-khus and fry again for 1 minute.
5. Remove from the fire and add the powdered masala and salt. Mix well.

How to proceed
1. Divide the dough into 4 portions.
2. Roll out one ball a little and put ½ tsp of filling in the centre. Lift the edges towards the centre and close the centre so as to completely envelope the stuffing. Roll again to make a 100 mm. (4") diameter paratha.
3. Repeat with the rest of the dough and stuffing to make 3 more parathas.
4. Cook on a non-stick pan until both sides are golden in colour.
5. Brush a little ghee on each paratha and serve hot.

Handy tip : Wheat germ is readily available at super markets, provision stores and also at chemist shops.

Nutritive values per paratha
Energy : 245 calories
Protein : 9.3 gm
Carbohydrate : 35.7 gm
Fat : 7.2 gm.
Zinc : 1.4 mg
Iron : 4.3 mg
Vitamin E : 2.1 mg

✳ *Spinach and Carrot Rice* ✳

Picture on page 55.

S*pinach and carrot layered with rice.... this recipe is doing wonders for hair with its high calcium and iron content.*

Preparation time : 20 minutes.   Cooking time : 10 minutes.
Baking temperature : 220°C (450°F).   Baking time : 25 minutes.   Serves 4.

For the rice layer
1 cup long-grained rice
½ tsp cumin seeds (jeera)
1 tsp oil
salt to taste

For the spinach layer
2¼ cups chopped spinach (palak)
¾ cup boiled green peas
3 green chillies, chopped
½ cup chopped onions
1 tsp oil

44

salt to taste

For the carrot layer
1½ cups grated carrot
½ tsp shah-jeera (caraway seeds)
1 tsp coriander (dhania) powder
¼ tsp cumin seed (jeera) powder
1 tsp oil
salt to taste

For baking
2 tbsp grated cooking cheese (optional)

For the rice layer
1. Cook the rice in boiling salted water till it is almost done. Each grain of the cooked rice should be separate. Drain and discard the water. Keep the rice aside.
2. Heat the oil in a vessel and fry the shah-jeera for a little time. Add the cooked rice and salt and mix gently.

For the spinach layer
1. Cook the spinach with 1 tbsp of water. When cooked, drain the spinach.

2. Heat the oil in a vessel and fry the onions for a little time. Add the spinach, green peas, chillies and salt and mix well.

For the carrot layer
1. Heat the oil in a vessel and fry the shah-jeera.
2. Add the grated carrot and 2 tbsp of water. Add the curry powder and salt and mix well. Cover and cook for a few minutes.

How to proceed
1. Grease a baking dish and spread half the cooked rice. Next spread the spinach mixture, cover with the remaining rice and finally with the carrot layer. Sprinkle the cheese on top.
2. Bake in a hot oven at 220°C (450°F) for 20 minutes.
   Serve hot.

Nutritive values per serving
Energy : 93 calories
Protein : 4.0 gm
Carbohydrate : 11.6 gm
Fat : 3.4 gm.
Calcium : 86.7 mg
Iron : 1.4 mg

For Bright Vision

Bright, sparkling eyes with a clear vision say so much for our youthful looks, besides being a big asset in leading an active life. Vision health benefits from good nutrition and regular exercise regime.

- Topping the list of necessary nutrients is **vitamin A**. A sure way of getting an adequate supply of this vitamin is by consuming enough fruits and vegetables containing beta-carotene, which gets converted into *'retinal'*, a form of vitamin A. A combination of retinal and a protein called *'opsin'* produces *'rhodopsin'*, a major pigment in the retina of the eye that contributes to good vision.
- To help vitamin A in its functions and also to keep the eye muscles working at their best, we need a good amount of **proteins**.
- Though vision is created when light enters our eyes, this same light produces some chemicals that could damage the eye. What protects our eyes from such damage is **vitamin C**.
- B-complex vitamins keep the skin around the eyes smooth and supple, so that there are no give-away signs of ageing, like crows feet.
- **Vitamin E** helps form new blood vessels and cuts down the risk of suffering from eye disorders.
- Among the minerals, **iron** plays an important role in the circulation of blood to the eye tissues.
- **Zinc** protects the eyes from infections.
- **Selenium,** an antioxidant, prevents the eye tissues from getting damaged.

That's surely a lot of nutrients that our eyes need! Of course, you don't have to worry about where you will get all these nutrients if you just follow these simple, easy-to-cook recipes.

❋ Carrot and Cheese Sandwich ❋

Munch on this innovative and nutritious cheesy carrot sandwich to get your share of vitamin A and iron.

Preparation time : 15 minutes.   No cooking.   Makes 2 sandwiches.

4 brown bread slices
2 tsp butter

To be mixed together for the filling
¾ cup grated carrots
2 tbsp grated mozarella cheese
2 tbsp grated paneer (cottage cheese)
1 tbsp milk
¼ tsp mustard (rai) powder
½ tsp chopped green chillies
salt to taste

1. Spread half the filling on a slice of bread.

2. Top with another slice of bread to make a sandwich.
3. Repeat with remaining filling and bread slices to make one more sandwich.
4. Cut each sandwich into two and serve.

Nutritive values per sandwich
Energy : 220 calories
Protein : 8.6 gm
Carbohydrate : 31.4 gm
Fat : 6.5 gm
Vitamin A : 736.3 mcg
Iron : 2.4 mg

✷ Fig and Apricot Shake ✷

Milk, rich in folic acid and vitamin B_2 blended with figs and apricot for all those who need good eyes.

Preparation time : a few minutes.   No cooking.   Makes 1 glass.

5 dried figs
4 dried apricots, deseeded
1 cup warm milk
4 to 5 ice-cubes

1. Soak the figs and apricots in warm milk for at least ½ hour.
2. Combine the milk and dried fruits in a liquidiser along with the ice-cubes and blend.
   Serve immediately.

Nutrient values per glass
Energy : 284 calories
Protein : 9.2 gm
Carbohydrates : 21.5 gm
Fat : 10.2 gm
Folic acid : 11.2 mcg
Vitamin B_2 : 0.2 mg

✳ *Rajma Cheese Parathas* ✳

A *mouth-watering recipe loaded with protein, iron and zinc is the best way to give all that your eyes need.*

Preparation time : 15 minutes.   Cooking time : 40 minutes.   Makes 4 parathas.

For the dough
1 cup whole wheat flour (gehun ka atta)
salt to taste

For the rajma filling
¼ cup (rajma) red kidney beans, soaked overnight
½ cup chopped onions
1 tsp grated ginger
1 large clove garlic, chopped
½ cup chopped tomatoes
¼ tsp turmeric powder (haldi)
1 tsp chilli powder
1 tsp coriander (dhania) powder

¼ cup fresh curds (dahi)
1 tbsp chopped coriander
1 tsp oil
salt to taste

Other ingredients
2 to 3 spring onions (including greens), finely chopped
3 tbsp grated cheese
2 tsp oil for cooking

For the dough
1. Combine all the ingredients and knead into a soft dough using enough water.
2. Divide the dough into 4 equal portions.
3. Roll out each portion into a 200 mm. (8") diameter circular chapati.
4. Cook each chapati lightly on both sides on a hot tava (griddle) and keep aside.

For the rajma filling
1. Drain the rajma, add 2 cups of water and pressure cook for 4 to 5 whistles till the rajma is overcooked.
2. Drain any excess liquid and keep aside.
3. Heat the oil in a pan, add the onions, ginger and garlic and sauté till the onions are

light brown in colour.
4. Add the tomatoes, turmeric powder, chilli powder, coriander powder and salt and cook till the oil separates.
5. Add the cooked rajma and mix well.
6. Add the curds and continue cooking till the mixture is dry.
7. Add the coriander and mix well. Keep aside to cool slightly. Divide into 4 equal portions.

How to proceed
1. Place one chapati on a dry surface and spread one portion of the rajma filling in the centre of the chapati.
2. Sprinkle some spring onions and ¾ tbsp of cheese.
3. Bring in all sides of the chapati towards the centre to enclose the filling and make a square paratha.
4. Seal the edges with a little water.
5. Repeat to make 3 more parathas.
6. Cook on both sides, using a little oil till the parathas are golden brown.
   Serve hot.

SPINACH AND CARROT RICE : Recipe on page 44 →

Nutritive values per paratha
Energy : 208 calories
Protein : 8.2 gm
Carbohydrate : 28.3 gm
Fat : 6.8 gm
Iron : 2.7 mg
Zinc : 1.2 mg

✻ *Hara Bhara Kebab* ✻

Picture on cover.

Vitamin E and folic acid rich spinach added to these delicious kebabs doing wonders for your eyes.

Preparation time : 10 minutes.   Cooking time : 20 minutes.   Makes 6 kebabs.

2 tbsp chana dal (split Bengal gram)
12 mm. (½") piece ginger
2 cloves garlic, grated
2 green chillies, finely chopped
½ cup spinach (palak), blanched, drained and roughly chopped
¼ cup boiled green peas
¼ cup grated paneer (cottage cheese)
½ tsp chaat masala
¼ tsp garam masala
salt to taste

Other ingredients
3 tbsp whole wheat bread crumbs

1 tsp oil for cooking

1. Pressure cook the chana dal, ginger, garlic and green chillies with ¾ cup of water for 2 to 3 whistles or until the dal is cooked. Drain out and discard any excess water.
2. Combine the spinach, green peas and cooked dal mixture and blend to a coarse paste without using any water.
3. Add the paneer, chaat masala and garam masala and mix well.
4. Divide the mixture into 6 equal portions and shape them into flat kebabs.
5. Roll the kebabs in the bread crumbs.
6. Heat the oil in a non-stick pan and cook the kebabs on both sides till they are golden brown in colour.
   Serve hot.

Nutritive values per kebab
Energy : 68 calories
Protein : 4.1 gm
Carbohydrate : 9.8 gm
Fat : 1.4 gm
Folic Acid: 43.2 mcg
Vitamin E: 0.6 mcg

* Golden Punch *

Here's a nutritious punch for stocking vitamin A and C stores needed for protecting your eyes from harmful substances causing infections.

Preparation time : a few minutes.   No cooking.   Makes 2 glasses.

2 cups chopped mango
1 cup chopped pineapple
½ tsp lemon juice
2 tsp sugar

To serve
mint sprigs and ice cubes

1. Mix all ingredients together in a blender and blend to a smooth purée.
2. Add 1 cup of water and mix well.
    Serve immediately with mint sprigs and ice cubes.

Nutritive values per glass
Energy : 116 calories
Protein : 0.9 gm
Carbohydrate : 26.8 gm
Fat : 0.6 gm
Vitamin A : 1980.4 mcg
Vitamin C : 22.9 mg

❋ *Aloo Paneer Chaat* ❋

Picture on back cover.

Snack on this lip-smacking, easy to cook chaat, which serves as a protein and calcium booster for your eyes.

Preparation time : 10 minutes. Cooking time : 15 minutes. Serves 6.

2 cups paneer (cottage cheese), cut into cubes
10 to 12 baby potatoes, boiled
1 cup boiled green peas
25 mm. (1") piece ginger
2 to 3 green chillies, finely chopped
2 tsp dry mango powder (amchur)
½ tsp freshly crushed pepper
1 tsp lemon juice
1 tbsp oil
salt to taste

For the garnish
2 tbsp chopped coriander

1. Heat the oil in a non-stick pan and add the green chilles and ginger and sauté for 1 minute.
2. Add the paneer, potatoes and green peas and cook for another minute.
3. Add the amchur, crushed pepper, lemon juice and salt and mix well.
4. Serve hot garnished with the chopped coriander.

Nutritive values per serving
Energy : 222 calories
Protein : 8.9 gm
Carbohydrate : 16.0 gm
Fat : 9.6 gm
Calcium : 241.6 mg

❈ Chick Pea and Soya Tikkis ❈

Picture on page 65.

Tikki, a traditional Indian snack, made healthy and nutritious to strengthen your eye muscles with its vitamin B_1 and zinc rich ingredients.

Preparation time : 10 minutes.   Cooking time : 10 minutes.   Makes 4 tikkis.

½ cup chick peas (kabuli chana), boiled and drained
½ cup soya granules
1 tbsp finely chopped mint
1 tsp finely chopped green chillies
1 tsp finely chopped ginger
1 tsp oil
salt to taste

1. Soak the soya granules in hot water for 10 to 15 minutes. Drain and squeeze out all the water.
2. Blend together the chick peas, soya nuggets and mint, in a blender to a smooth paste.
3. Add the green chillies, ginger, salt and mix well.

63

4. Divide the mixture into 4 equal portions and shape into round, flat tikkis.
5. Cook them on a non-stick pan using a little oil till both sides are golden brown. Serve hot with a chutney of your choice.

Nutritive values per tikki
Energy : 77 calories
Protein : 4.6 gm
Carbohydrate : 7.7 gm
Fat : 3.1 gm
Vitamin B_1 : 0.1 mg
Zinc : 0.6 mg

CHICK PEA AND SOYA TIKKIS : Recipe on page 63 →

✳ *Papaya Pineapple Juice* ✳

Picture on page 75.

An unusual combination of vitamin C rich pineapple and vitamin A rich papaya would surely do wonders for your eyes.

Preparation time : a few minutes.   No cooking.   Makes 2 glasses.

2 cups papaya, cut into cubes
1 cup pineapple, cut into cubes
a few ice-cubes

1. Blend the all ingredients together in a blender along with ¼ cup of water to a smooth purée.
2. Pour into 2 tall glasses and serve immediately.

Nutritive values per glass

Energy : 83 calories	Protein : 1.2 gm	Carbohydrate : 19.0 gm
Fat : 0.2 gm	Vitamin C : 82.2 mg	Vitamin A : 947.3 mcg

For Healthy Bones

Much as the strength of a building depends on a sound structure, our bodies too need a strong frame in order to be healthy. Hence, it is so very necessary that we take care of our bone health by eating right, if we are to remain youthful and active throughout our life.

- **Proteins** are needed for maintaining bone strength and for repairing damaged tissues. However, compared to young children, protein needs fall as we get older

- A **calcium-rich diet** is the most important part of any regimen for the care of bones. Calcium is also essential for the teeth, and helps to keep them intact so that we can not only eat well, but also give those winning smiles that proclaim our youthfulness.

- Helping the body to absorb the calcium is **vitamin D**, which also assists in maintaining adequate levels of this mineral in the blood. So we need plenty of vitamin D too.

- Also helping the absorption of calcium is **vitamin C**, which, additionally, strengthens both bones and muscle. Because of its immunity-boosting properties, vitamin C helps in the healing of broken bones too.

- **Vitamin A**, **magnesium** and **zinc** also play a role in building a healthy bone structure.

❅ *Paneer Pasanda* ❅

Picture on page 2.

This simple and delicious paneer recipe for all those who want to pop up their muscles with protein.

Preparation time : 15 minutes.   Cooking time : 20 minutes.   Serves 4.

1½ cups paneer (cottage cheese), cut into cubes
¼ cup milk
¼ cup fresh curds (dahi)
½ tsp Bengal gram flour (besan)
½ tsp cumin seeds (jeera)
¼ tsp kasuri methi (dried fenugreek leaves)
¼ tsp garam masala
½ cup chopped coriander
1 tsp oil
salt to taste

For the paste
1¼ cups sliced onions

¼ cup finely chopped cauliflower
1 to 2 green chillies
12 mm. (½") piece ginger, sliced
1 stick cinnamon (dalchini)
1 clove (laung)
1 cup milk

For the paste
1. Combine all the ingredients in a pan and simmer for 8 to 10 minutes till the onions are soft and nearly all the liquid has evaporated. Cool.
2. Purée the mixture to a smooth paste in a blender. Keep aside.

How to proceed
1. Combine the milk, curds and gram flour and whisk well. Keep aside.
2. Heat the oil in a non-stick pan, add the cumin seeds, kasuri methi and the prepared paste and sauté for 2 to 3 minutes.
3. Add the curds and gram flour mixture, garam masala and salt and bring to a boil.
4. Add the paneer and coriander and mix well.
   Serve hot.

Nutritive values per serving
Energy : 217 calories
Protein : 9.1 gm
Carbohydrate : 8.5 gm
Fat : 13.3 gm.
Calcium : 209.5 mg

❉ *Broccoli and Walnut Soup* ❉

Vitamin C rich ingredient - broccoli, doing wonders for your bones by enhancing protein absorption.

Preparation time : 10 minutes.   Cooking time : 15 minutes.   Serves 4.

2 cups chopped broccoli florets and stems
¼ cup chopped onions
1 medium potato, boiled and peeled
1 cup milk
1 tbsp oil
salt and freshly crushed pepper to taste

For the garnish
2 tbsp chopped walnuts

1. Heat the oil in a pan and sauté the onions lightly.
2. Add the broccoli and cook gently for a few minutes.
3. Add 3 cups of water and cook until the broccoli is done.

4. Pass through a blender along with the boiled potato and make a purée.
5. Add the milk, salt and pepper and mix well.
   Serve hot.

Nutritive values per serving
Energy : 149 calories.
Protein : 4.5 gm
Carbohydrate : 9.3 gm.
Fat : 9.4 gm.
Vitamin C : 27.7 mg

❋ *Chana Kofta Kadhi* ❋

Traditional kadhi made nutritious with chick pea koftas that serves as a wealth of protein and calcium to strengthen your bones.

Preparation time : 15 minutes.   Cooking time : 20 minutes.   Serves 4.

For the kadhi
2 cups fresh curds (dahi)
1 tbsp Bengal gram flour (besan)
1 green chilli, finely chopped
1 tsp grated ginger
½ tsp cumin seeds (jeera)
1 stick cinnamon (dalchini)
¼ tsp asafoetida (hing)
salt to taste

For the chana koftas
⅓ cup chick peas (kabuli chana), soaked overnight
½ cup chopped coriander

½ cup chopped fenugreek (methi) leaves
¼ cup chopped spinach (palak)
1 green chilli, chopped
salt to taste

For the kadhi
1. Combine the curds, gram flour and 1 cup of water and whisk well. Keep aside.
2. Pound the green chilli, ginger together in a mortar and pestle. Keep aside.
3. Heat the oil in a pan and add the cumin seeds, cinnamon and asafoetida.
4. When the cumin seeds crackle, add the curds and gram flour mixture, prepared green chilli mixture and salt and simmer for 5 to 10 minutes. Keep aside.

For the chana koftas
1. Drain the chick peas.
2. Grind all the ingredients to a fine paste in a blender without using water.
3. Divide the mixture into 20 equal portions and shape each portion into an even sized round. Keep aside.

STRAWBERRY NECTAR : Recipe on page 88 ⟶
PAPAYA PINEAPPLE JUICE : Recipe on page 66 ⟶

How to proceed
1. Re-heat the kadhi and bring it to a boil.
2. Drop the prepared koftas in the boiling kadhi and allow them to simmer for 5 to 10 minutes.
   Serve hot.

Handy tip : If the kofta mixture is difficult to shape into rounds, you may need to add 1 tbsp Bengal gram flour (besan) to the mixture and mix well.

Nutritive values per serving
Energy : 175 calories
Protein : 6.2 gm
Carbohydrate : 10.8 gm
Fat : 9.5 gm
Calcium : 246.5 mg

❈ *Soya Mutter ki Subzi* ❈

Picture on page 85.

A *great way to sneak in protein and calcium packed soya nuggets in your diet.*

Preparation time : 10 minutes.   Cooking time : 40 minutes.   Serves 4.

½ cup soya nuggets
¾ cup boiled green peas
½ tsp cumin seeds (jeera)
a pinch asafoetida (hing)
1 tsp ginger-green chilli paste
½ tsp garlic paste
½ cup chopped onions
½ cup finely chopped tomatoes
¼ tsp turmeric powder (haldi)
½ tsp chilli powder
½ tsp coriander (dhania) powder
¼ cup fresh curds (dahi)
2 tsp Bengal gram flour (besan)
2 tbsp milk

½ tsp sugar
2 tsp oil
salt to taste

1. Cook the soya nuggets in hot salted water for about 20 minutes. Squeeze out the water and keep aside.
2. Heat the oil in a non-stick pan and add the cumin seeds. When they crackle, add the asafoetida, ginger-green chilli paste, garlic paste and onions and sauté till the onions turn translucent.
3. Add the tomatoes, turmeric powder, chilli powder and coriander powder and cook on a slow flame for about 5 to 10 minutes.
4. Mix the curds, gram flour, milk and ¾ cup of water and add to the onion-tomato gravy.
5. Add the soya nuggets, green peas, sugar and salt and simmer for 2 more minutes. Serve hot.

Handy tip : You can use mushrooms or paneer instead of the soya nuggets as a variation.

Nutritive values per serving
Energy : 134 calories
Protein : 7.8 gm
Carbohydrate : 11.7 gm
Fat : 5.8 gm
Calcium : 86.6 mg

❊ Methi Palak Dhoklas ❊

D*hoklas enriched with protein and vitamin C is a classic snack for your child's growing bones.*

Preparation time : 10 minutes.   Cooking time : 20 minutes.   Serves 4.

1 cup black-eyed beans (chawli)
¾ cup chopped spinach (palak)
¾ cup chopped fenugreek (methi) leaves
1 tbsp green chilli-ginger paste
1½ tsp asafoetida (hing)
1 tbsp fruit salt
2 tbsp oil
salt to taste

For Serving
green chutney

1. Wash and soak the beans for at least 6 hours. Drain.

2. Add approx. ¾ cup of water and blend in a liquidiser to make a smooth batter.
3. Add the spinach, fenugreek, oil, green chilli-ginger paste, asafoetida and salt and mix well into a batter.
4. Put the steamer on the gas and when the water in the steamer starts to boil, add the fruit salt into the batter and mix well.
5. Pour the batter into 3 greased thalis, put them in the steamer and steam for 8 to 10 minutes.
Serve hot with green chutney.

Handy tips : 1. Add the fruit salt into the batter just before you are ready to steam the dhoklas, or the dhoklas will not rise.
2. Remember that the water in the steamer should be boiling when you put in the dhoklas to steam.

Nutritive values per serving
Energy : 120 calories
Protein : 6.5 gm
Carbohydrate : 14.2 gm
Fat : 4.1 gm
Vitamin C : 6.3 mg

* Three Bean Salad *

This calcium and protein packed bean salad is for those who want to make up for their lost muscle mass.

Preparation time : 20 minutes.   No cooking.   Serves 4.

¼ cup boiled rajma (kidney beans)
½ cup boiled chick peas (kabuli chana)
½ cup boiled butter beans (lima beans or pavta)
2 spring onions, finely chopped
1 tomato, deseeded and cut into small cubes
¼ cup mozzarella cheese or cheese, cut into 12 mm. (½") cubes
1 cup iceberg lettuce, torn into pieces

To be mixed into a dressing
1 tbsp olive oil
¼ tsp dried oregano
salt and freshly ground pepper to taste
¼ tsp chopped garlic

1. Combine all the ingredients except the dressing in a salad bowl. Toss well. Chill for at least 2 to 3 hours.
2. Just before serving, toss the dressing in the salad.
   Serve immediately.

Nutritive values per serving
Energy : 206 calories
Protein : 11.2 gm
Carbohydrate : 25.0 gm
Fat : 6.9 gm
Calcium : 140.0 mg

✳ *Pineapple Banana Yoghurt Shake* ✳

Here's a calcium and vitamin C rich fruity shake....sure to appeal your child's palate and bones too!

Preparation time : a few minutes.   No cooking.   Makes 2 tall glasses.

¾ cup fresh curds (dahi)
¾ cup chopped pineapple
½ ripe banana
4 tsp sugar
3 ice-cubes

For the garnish
a few mint sprigs

SOYA MUTTER KI SUBZI : Recipe on page 77 ➜

1. Blend the yoghurt, pineapple, banana, sugar and ½ teacup of water in a liquidiser.
2. Pour into tall glasses, top with crushed ice and garnish with mint sprigs.
   Serve immediately.

Nutritive values per glass
Energy : 90 calories
Protein : 2.3 gm
Carbohydrate : 19.7 gm
Fat : 0.2 gm
Vitamin C : 28.1 mg
Calcium : 106.0 mg

To Increase Immunity

We owe much to our body's wonderful immune system for fighting off illness and keeping us in good health. Supporting our immune system through healthy dietary and lifestyle choices will help to boost its fighting power.

Certain nutrients in food are especially effective in building up resistance...

- **Vitamins C and E** is at the top of the list as they contain antioxidants that counteract the harmful cellular by-products created during normal metabolism. Though oxygen is an essential element for life, it can create these damaging by-products that affect the immune system.
- Also, eating enough of vegetables that are rich in beta-carotene can ensure that our bodies get enough of **vitamin A** to mop up the damaging molecules that speed-up ageing.
- Very necessary for the production and maintenance of the infection-fighting cells is **protein**.
- Among the minerals, **zinc** is vital for increasing the production and also the effectiveness of cells that fight viral infections.

These tried and tested recipes containing infection preventing and immunity-boosting foods will help to keep our immune systems at their peak operating efficiency.

✳ *Strawberry Nectar* ✳

Picture on page 75.

Vitamin C laden recipe not only boosts up your immune system but also gives a glow to your skin.

Preparation time : a few minutes.   No cooking.   Makes 2 glasses.

1 cup strawberry purée
2 tbsp lemon juice
2 tbsp sugar
10 to12 ice-cubes

For the garnish
a few strawberry slices

1. Blend all the ingredients together in a liquidiser with 1 cup of water.
2. Pour into in 2 tall glasses and serve immediately garnished with strawberry slices.

Nutritive values per glass
Energy : 90 calories
Protein : 0.7 gm
Carbohydrate : 20.9 gm
Fat : 0.3 gm
Vitamin C : 44.9 mg

* Peach Satin *

Vitamin C boost poured in to a glass should be one's choice to fight infections and common cold.

Preparation time : a few minutes.   No cooking.   Makes 2 glasses.

¼ cup pineapple juice
¾ cup orange juice
½ cup sliced peach
a few ice-cubes

For the garnish
1 tbsp whipped cream

To decorate
1 cherry
1 lemon slice

1. Put all the ingredients in a blender for a few seconds.
2. Pour in a tall glass. Top with ice-cubes.
   Serve decorated with a cherry and a lemon slice.

Nutritive values per glass
Energy : 76 calories
Protein : 1.1 gm
Carbohydrate : 14.9 gm
Fat : 1.3 gm
Vitamin C : 76.2 mg

❄ *Melon Tango* ❄

Vitamin A rich muskmelon blended creatively with vitamin C rich orange juice and coconut water to make a relishing immune booster.

Preparation time : 5 minutes.   No cooking.   Makes 4 glasses.

2 cups muskmelon (kharbooja), cut into cubes
juice of 2 oranges
2 cups tender coconut water
2 tsp sugar
a pinch black salt (sanchal)

For the garnish
a few mint leaves

1. Blend the melon in a liquidiser. Strain it.
2. Combine all the ingredients and mix well.
3. Serve chilled poured into glasses and garnished with mint leaves.

Handy tip : To reduce the amount of sugar required, use a ripe muskmelon.

Nutritive values for one glass
Energy : 89 calories
Protein : 2.2 gm
Carbohydrates : 19.1 gm
Fat : 0.4 gm
Vitamin A : 1098.2 mcg
Vitamin C : 47.9 mg

❋ Sweet Lime and Pepper Salad ❋

Full of flavour and colour, this crunchy salad is best to build up your immunity with its vitamin C and A rich ingredients like lettuce and capsicum.

Preparation time : 10 minutes.   No cooking.   Serves 3.

1 cup sweet lime segments
1 cup chopped yellow and green capsicum
2 cups lettuce, torn into pieces
1 cup cucumber cubes

To be mixed into a dressing
½ tsp mustard (rai) powder
½ tsp pepper powder
juice of 1 lemon
salt to taste

1. Combine all the ingredients for the salad in a bowl and chill.
2. Just before serving, pour the dressing over the salad and toss well.

Serve immediately.

Nutritive values per serving:
Energy : 66 calories
Protein : 3.5 gm
Carbohydrates : 11.5 gm
Fat : 0.7 gm
Vitamin A : 1229.6 mcg
Vitamin C : 82.6 mg

* Melon and Papaya Scoops in Honey Ginger Dressing *

Picture on page 1.

Vitamin A rich papaya and melon scoops tossed together in an unusual zinc rich honey ginger dressing to enhance your immunity.

Preparation time : 15 minutes.   No cooking.   Serves 6.

1½ cups papaya scoops (preferably the red variety)
1½ cups muskmelon (kharbooja) scoops
1½ cups watermelon scoops

To be blended into a honey-ginger dressing
2 tbsp honey
1 tbsp lemon juice
2 tsp ginger juice
¼ tsp crushed pepper
salt to taste

For the garnish
mint sprigs

1. Arrange the scooped fruits in a bowl, pour the dressing and toss gently.
2. Refrigerate till chill and serve garnished with mint sprigs.

Nutritive values per serving
Energy : 45 calories
Protein : 0.6 gm
Carbohydrate : 10.7 gm
Fat : 0.2 gm
Vitamin A : 296.5 mcg
Zinc : 0.7 mg

* Spicy Sprouts Sandwich *

An unusual way of making a sandwich nutritious with protein and zinc laden sprouts.

Preparation time : 10 minutes.   Cooking time : 20 minutes.   Makes 4 sandwiches.

8 slices whole wheat bread
½ cup sliced onions
4 tsp low fat butter to cook

For the sprouts
1 cup mixed sprouts, boiled
½ cup potatoes, boiled and mashed
½ cup finely chopped onions
2 tsp ginger-garlic paste
1 green chilli, finely chopped
2 tsp pav bhaji masala
2 tsp coriander-cumin seed (dhania-jeera) powder
¼ tsp turmeric powder (haldi)

½ tsp black salt (sanchal)
1½ cups finely chopped tomatoes
2 tsp oil
salt to taste

For the sprouts
1. Heat the oil in a non-stick pan, add the onions and sauté till the onions turn translucent.
2. Add the ginger-garlic paste, green chilli and sauté for another 1 minute.
3. Add the pav bhaji masala, coriander-cumin seed powder, turmeric powder, black salt, tomatoes and salt and cook for 5 minutes.
4. Add the sprouts and potatoes and mix well. Keep aside.

How to proceed
1. Divide the sprouts mixture into 4 equal portions.
2. Place one portion on one slice of bread. Top with an onion slice and sandwich using another slice of bread.
3. Repeat with the remaining ingredients to make 3 more sandwiches.
4. Pre-heat the griller and grill the sandwiches, using a little low fat butter to cook. Serve hot.

Handy tip : Pav bhaji masala is a spice blend that is easily available at provision
stores.

Nutritive values per sandwich
Energy : 220 calories
Protein : 8.4 gm
Carbohydrates : 34.7 gm
Fat : 5.2 gm
Zinc : 0.7 mg

❋ *Coriander Rotis* ❋

*C*oriander not only lends a delicious flavour to these rotis but also increases its Vitamin A and C content.

Preparation time : 20 minutes.   Cooking time : 30 minutes.   Makes 6 rotis.

For the dough
1½ cups whole wheat flour (gehun ka atta)
½ tsp salt

To be mixed into a stuffing
1 cup chopped coriander
2 tsp coriander-cumin seed (dhania-jeera) powder
¼ tsp turmeric powder (haldi)
1 tbsp Bengal gram flour (besan)
3 green chillies, finely chopped
salt to taste

Other ingredients
1 tbsp oil for brushing

For the dough
1. Mix all the ingredients and add enough water to make a semi-stiff dough.
2. Knead well and divide into 6 equal portions.
3. Roll out each portion into a thick round with the help of the flour.

How to proceed
1. Divide the stuffing into 6 equal portions.
2. Brush each dough round with a little oil and spread one stuffing portion on it.
3. Roll out into a cigar shape.
4. Make a small round like a coil and press lightly by hand.
5. Roll out again into a thick roti.
6. Repeat for the remaining dough and stuffing to make 5 more rotis.
7. Cook on a hot tawa (griddle) until pink spots appear on both the sides.
8. Brush a little oil on top and serve hot.

Nutritive values per roti
Energy : 121 calories
Protein : 3.7 gm
Carbohydrates : 19.8 gm
Fat : 3.1 gm
Vitamin A : 320.3 mcg
Vitamin C : 5.6 mg

Total Health Series by Tarla Dalal

The Total Health series is a range of cookbooks specially designed and carefully researched by a team of qualified nutritionists. These books are an action-oriented guide for good health and wellness to suit the nutritional needs for different age groups, be it an expectant mum, a baby, an individual who has a medical problem or aims to lose weight. These books will help you and your family stay in fine fettle. They have opened new vistas in the field of cooking while providing you with healthy guidelines for adding verve and vitality to your life. Some of the titles in this series are:

Low Calorie Healthy Cooking

Pregnancy Cook Book

Baby & Toddler Cook Book

Healthy Heart Cook Book

Cooking with 1 Teaspoon of Oil

Delicious Diabetic Recipes